AS SOMEONE DIES

As Someone Dies

a handbook for the living

Elizabeth Johnson

HAY
HOUSE

Dedication

With special appreciation to Kim.
This book is for my Mother.

"Death puts Life into perspective."

—EMERSON

Stripped of all purple robes,
Stripped of all golden lies,
I will not be afraid,
Truth will persevere through death.

—JOHN MASEFIELD

Contents

Introduction

by Louise L. Hay, D. D.

Shortly after I published my last book, *I Love My Body*, in 1985, I knew it was time to expand the library and bring in the works of other authors who support my philosophy of life. Two weeks after the decision God brought Elizabeth Johnson to me.

At this time, with the increase of cancer and now AIDS, many more people are leaving the planet. Some of them are quite young, and there is a greater need for understanding the process of death. No longer can we hide our heads and pretend death does not exist.

Elizabeth truly understands that death is another experience of life. She is there for us in those times of need with practical suggestions. I have used some of them myself when visiting those who are seriously ill. There may come a time when we need to be able to say to a loved one: "Its all right to go, you can leave now." Elizabeth helps us to say this without guilt. There is much wisdom in this book, and it can be read at any time by anyone.

I am very pleased to present Elizabeth Johnson's work as one of the first publishing projects at Hay House. The beauty and gentleness expressed in *As Someone Dies* will be a comfort for many.

—Santa Monica, September 2, 1986

And when he shall die
take him
and cut him out in little stars
and he will make the face of heaven
so fine
that all the world
will be in love with the night
and pay no worship
to the garish sun.

—WILLIAM SHAKESPEARE
Romeo and Juliet

Foreword

Death is not unusual. Every single person in the entire world will, one day, leave the earth, make the transition, expire, pass over, pass on, graduate, die. It is as normal and natural as birth. Both a universal act and a very personal experience.

While the loved one (anyone with whom we are spending this precious time) is busily involved in the dying process, the rest of us are saddened, angered, confused, nervous, and sometimes even embarrassed witnessing the intimacy of the procedure. We will ourselves to be there, yet stand by, feeling helpless. What can I do/say to help . . ., and, what if I do/say the wrong thing?

The double-edged sword: so immersed in our own fears, we emotionally pull back from the dying, and so concerned with the dying, we neglect our own nurturing.

Many fine books have been written on the subject of death and dying; some are listed here under Recommended Reading. The subject of "death education" is advancing rapidly, with a broad spectrum of scientists, psychologists, teachers/counselors, philosophers, doctors/nurses who are researching, questioning, learning about the death, near-death, and after-death experience. They quest to understand and pass on that understanding to eliminate the most basic of human fears—the fear of not being here any longer.

Yet, when the immediate experience centers on *your* loved one, theories are hard to remember and books seem to hold little meaning.

This handbook is designed for you to *use:* 1) during the stressful days of a loved one's impending death; 2) after the death, to allow grief to heal the sense of loss; and 3) to build a better understanding of death as it pertains to life.

Through the entire process, whether it is called death or transition, it is important to remember that each of us is composed of four elements: body, mind, emotions, and Life Force. The one who is passing away is not just his/her body; just as you, during this very emotional time, are not just your feelings.

This handbook has been written to assist all of us.

It has been especially influenced by the lives of:

Charles J. Johnson	1909-1974
Thomas L. Johnson	1943-1983
Mr. Max Whiteshoes	1980-1982

AS SOMEONE DIES

God is not a God of the dead, but of the living, for in his sight, all are alive. The Spirit is both birthless and deathless. The Principle of Life cannot know death. The experience of dying is but the laying off of an old garment, and the donning of a new one. There are bodies celestial and bodies terrestrial, there is a material body and a spiritual body. This spiritual body is the resurrection body.

—ERNEST HOLMES
The Science of Mind

1

Life

Brain And Mind, Body And Soul

With excerpts from Ralph Waldo Emerson's essay,
"The Over-Soul"

> *"We see the world piece by piece, as the sun,the*
> *moon, the animal, the tree; but the Whole, of*
> *which these are the shining parts, is the Soul."*

As members of the human race, we primarily perceive life through our senses. We get our information about people, places, things, and events from what we see, hear, touch, taste, smell; *i.e.,* from what we witness and experience as we move through the days of our lives.

We are receptors, or receivers, of information and data about what is going on around us and around the world. This, to a high degree, helps to form what we think of as our "self;" that is, our "beingness" including personality, thoughts, emotions, actions, reactions, and our general outlook on life. In other words, the information we receive from our senses helps to form who we think we "are."

Since you are reading this book, you *are*. You exist. You know that you exist because you see the words, feel the paper, hear sounds around you, perhaps even smell dinner cooking. Simultaneously, your brain is quickly translating letters into words, into sentences, into meaning. Along with this, you are mentally registering other environmental stimuli and perhaps emotionally experiencing feelings of the past and present, or even projecting into the future. This, all happening automatically and at once, is quite remarkable.

You are even more remarkable.

> *"We live in succession, in division, in parts, in particles. Meanwhile, within man is the soul of the Whole; the wise silence, the universal beauty, to which every part and particle is equally related: the eternal ONE."*

We are all, equally, a part of the Eternal One. We are, in fact, not only a part of the Eternal One, but, also, the Eternal One lives and expresses through us, as us. While you are busy with your particular life on earth, the Eternal One (or Infinite Mind, or God) is, all the while, expressing Itself as you.

What does this mean? It means that you (and I) are so much more than we think or feel we are. We are each more than our thoughts, more than our feelings, more than our actions. We are each connected to the Infinite Mind, or God, or Eternal

One. The soul of each of us is the Soul of the Infinite Mind.

Now, the word, "soul," *(l'ame, psyche, el alma, ziel, kokoru, die Seele, sjel, l'anima)* is simply a term that seems to relate these days as much to music, food, and religion as it does to the Eternal, Infinite Mind. Yet the soul does express in each individual through, or as, the mind. You could say the mind is the soul, inspiring the person.

But where is the person's soul? It cannot be found in the physical body because it is not *of* the body, yet it operates the body.

Likewise, where is a person's mind? The mind cannot be found in the brain, yet the brain is a tool of the mind.

> *"A man is a facade of a temple wherein all wisdom and good abide."*

There is One Eternity, therefore, one Universal Mind, which is Eternal. Our individualized mind, as an expression of Universal Mind, is eternal. Our body is the temple of the mind/soul and, as matter, it is not eternal.

Our individual "being," is a result of Infinite Mind (*i.e.*, God) incarnating into the form of each and every one of us. This is creation. Just as Infinite Mind creates by thought, so do we. Since you, the person, are alive (and reading this material), you are also constantly creating through your thoughts. Thought creates. Life is a rich passage of ideas, feelings, sights, sounds, experiences, and all forms of communication. While *receiving* information and influences, you are also *creating* experiences (both challenging and rewarding) because Infinite Mind, of which your mind is an aspect, continually creates by thought. So do you.

When the activity of the brain ceases, mind moves on to further create. It does not simply die or go away. It cannot. Mind/soul, as part of the Infinite Intelligence of the Universe, is Eternal. You—the individualization of the Infinite—are Eternal. No soul can be damned or lost, just as no mind can die. The Infinite is far beyond even acknowledging that concept. The Infinite continues to create—and incarnate—Universally.

> *"The soul looketh steadily forwards, creating a world before her, leaving worlds behind her....*
> *The soul knows only the soul; the web of events is the flowing robe in which she is clothed."*

There is comfort here, and safety, and great love. The mind/soul leaves the body to move *forward.* The essence of each person moves into larger growth, into more multi-colored experiences, to incarnate again. The uniqueness of each of us continues in ways and spheres we do not now remember. Yet the essence continues to grow Eternally.

Now, I wish you to feel, and know, and be all the qualities of the Infinite that are found in you, in me, in everyone. This is the true essence of you. It never dies, and it is you forever more. Remarkable you:

Love   Light   Life   Peace
Power   Beauty   Joy

I put aside my concept of reality.
I am willing to trust that that
which now seems beyond my grasp,
is the unseen but certain Love,
which leads my beloved to his
perfect place.

"Applaud my friends, the comedy is over."

— Ludwig van Beethoven
(on his deathbed)

And now the time has come when we must depart; I to my death, you to go on living. But which of us is going to the better fate is unknown to all except God.

— Socrates

2

Before

Why?

Although it is impossible to fully answer the question "why?," it seems also impossible not to ask it. We want to know why this is happening to someone we love. We want to know why this is happening to *us*.

We may angrily shake our fists at the heavens, cry bitter tears at the pending loss, anesthetize ourselves with alcohol, valium, marijuana, whatever. The question remains: Why is the person I love dying? Why?

Write down the question. Keep a private, personal journal or diary, or use the blank pages in this book to write in. When you ask yourself "why?," truly ask yourself by writing both the question and what you feel to be the answer(s). Along with "I don't know," you will come up with many answers—and these answers can reveal to you closeted thoughts and feelings which, when written and examined (*i.e.*, realized) lose all their power and control over you.

These "answers" may include feelings of loss, betrayal, abandonment, punishment, fear, *etc.* Be sure to know that any feelings you have during this time are all right. There is nothing "wrong" with emotions and there is nothing "wrong" with you. You are not a bad person because you may feel fearful, angry, or vulnerable.

By using the question "why?" as a focus and writing your thoughts and feelings, you are doing a great service to yourself and the dying person. You are bringing to the hospital or sick bed a sense of clarity about yourself. And, although your feelings will alter and change as time goes on, you are showing love for all concerned by allowing yourself private moments to write down how you honestly feel. In doing this you are allowing yourself to express your thoughts outwardly, yet not verbally.

You need not share this writing with anyone, although you may if you wish. Be with yourself for a few moments each day, and write down your thoughts and feelings.

Hour By Hour

If there would be an "ideal" transition situation, it would probably be a very old person, gently slipping away, at home, surrounded and supported by loving family and friends.

More often, however, we are presented with a hospital or hospice environment, where we sit with a loved one for hours at a time, while they doze, fidget, or simply be themselves.

What does this time mean to you? And to them? It can provide some of the most memorable, meaningful hours in both your lives. It is not necessary to feel you must "do" anything—your physical presence shows your love.

Yet there are some things all of us can do.

Take your cue from the dying person. Allow the person to decide if he or she wants to talk or not; if not, then you do something for yourself— read the newspaper or a book; do needlepoint or crossword puzzles. Expression of thoughts and feelings is also up to them. Listen with interest. If the language is unintelligible, listen with interest anyway, because some communication *is* taking place.

Allow the person to feel very safe with you. Offer to hold their hand, stroke their arm, massage their hands and feet, comb their hair. The physical sensation of touching brings with it comfort and a sense of security. But ask or suggest first. The person may simply not be in the mood.

If there are moments when you just don't know what to say, smile and *think* the words you would *like* to say.

During this time, it is very important for you to be aware of your own needs. While your focus remains on the other person, it's fine to take a walk around the block or go to the cafeteria for awhile. Physical movement and changes in visual images will energize you and help to lessen stress and the feeling of being drained.

Whether you are with the person or not, take some time occasionally to run through your senses mentally. While the person naps, or perhaps as you go to/from the hospital, take each sense separately and mentally record what it is doing:

—What do you see? What color is the sky; what different shapes are the trees?

—Identify the sounds that you hear. How many different sounds are there in your immediate environment?

—What smells are present? Are they pleasant or not?

—Do you have a taste in your mouth? What is it?

—How does the breeze/sun/air feel on your skin?

—What are your hands touching and how does it feel to you?

This sense evaluation sharpens your awareness of the things around you and increases your own mental alertness.

The easiest thing for you to do for yourself during these hours is to be aware of your breathing. Slightly exaggerate inhaling and exhaling often. This increases oxygen in your system and aids in calming stressed nerves.

Although you may feel you can take care of yourself "later," doing these things for yourself now increases your immediate ability to endure and helps to provide a natural defense against depression. Know that the hours will pass.

The Other Person

Each death is as individual and unique as each life. Although we know that the Life Force (or Spirit, Soul, God, Source, Force, Energy, Infinite Mind, *i.e.*, the Thing that enlivens all things) withdraws from the body, we do not know exactly how. There is a different design, a different process for each individual.

When the terminally ill, distinguished, intelligent gentleman becomes cantankerous and abusive, it is simply part of his own individual process of letting go of this world.

Likewise, when the gentle, devoted wife and mother glares in angry, defiant aggression, it is one of the steps she must take to complete her life.

We do not really know why this happens, taking into account reactions to medication, but you may witness moments of total personality reversal in your loved one. Remember that this is a part of the person's unique dying process, and although it may be directed at you, it really has nothing to do with you. It is perhaps reaction to medication; it is perhaps reaction to inner anger and fear; or it is perhaps simply a step the loved one takes in their specific way of dying.

If the person is cranky, angry, or abusive, be both honest and fair: "I love you. And please don't speak to me that way."

In this manner, you are helping the person move through and get out of that stage of the process.

There may be times when the person seems to be "talking crazy," hallucinating, or going senile. He or she may speak of people, places, events as though everything were happening now. Or, in sleep, the person's hands may move busily, appearing to be directing traffic, hammering nails, counting money, etc.

The wonderful makeup of body, mind, emotions, and Life Force now enables the person to think, feel, and imagine on many different levels, in many different areas. Remember that what the person is saying and doing is very real to him/her. Due to a freer expression of the subconscious, the person may be speaking and acting out in symbols. These symbols, though foreign to you, have solid meaning to the loved one.

Rather than trying to coerce the person back to the "reality" of the hospital room or ignoring the ramblings (which is ignoring the person), try to play along.

In my own experience (see Chapter 3), my brother woke from a nap one afternoon and said:

"Honey, you've got to move your car."

"Why?" I asked.

"Because it's blocking the fire wall."

"Can't I move it later?"

"No, can't you see?" (He waved his arm in the direction of the television set.) "It's blocking the fire wall!"

"Okay, I'll move it now."

So I got up, walked out of the room, walked back into the room and said, "I moved the car."

"Thanks," he broadly smiled, "I really appreciate it."

It did him good to participate in a scene that made no sense to me but was vivid and real to him.

Also, be aware that the loved one, even when apparently asleep, can hear what is going on in the room. He or she is also very involved in the biggest adventure of life, equalled only by birth. So discourage a visiting Aunt Rosie from rattling on about her bridge club and say only what you would want your loved one to hear.

Quiet Moments

The finest communication is in our thought, and we can give ourselves the freedom not to speak at times.

Look at your loved one's hand. Hold it. Look at the skin, veins, nails. Appreciate it as being *a part* of the person you know.

Look at your loved one's face. Look at the structure, the color, the lines. Appreciate it as being *a part* of the person you know.

Scan down the bed and look at the outline of your loved one's body. Appreciate it as being *a part* of the person you know.

Now gently inhale and exhale four or five times. Look at your loved one and know—tell yourself—that what you are seeing is *a part* of the person you know.

Look beyond the body. Know that your loved one is eternal. Appreciate that. Know that *you* are eternal. Appreciate that. Breathe deeply.

Feeling Helpless

Watching someone die and being able to do nothing to prevent it takes an emotional toll. We may feel ourselves to be the victims of our own helplessness. Yet, by participating in the transformation process, by being there with the person, for the person, we are hardly helpless. We are helpers.

We may fluff pillows, hold hands, talk, listen, help with sips of water. We can do more.

1.   Either in the loved one's room or elsewhere, sit quietly and close your eyes. Be aware of your breathing. In your mind, select a color that represents to you comfort and safety. Whatever color you choose is fine. Now imagine that you can surround your loved one in this color. Imagine that you can see the person comfortably surrounded and protected by the color you have chosen. Hold this image in your mind and be aware that you are breathing. When it is comfortable for you, open your eyes.

2.   Select a piece of soothing classical or soft music that appeals to you. With the music playing, sit quietly and close your eyes. Be aware of your breathing. Now, imagine that you can direct each

note of music completely through the body of your loved one. Picture the person in your mind and imagine that each note of music travels through the body bringing tranquility, safety and comfort to every part of the person. Continue imagining this until the music ends. Be aware of your breathing and, when it is comfortable for you, open your eyes.

3. Whenever the whirlwind of thoughts and feelings seems to overwhelm you, sit quietly and close your eyes. Feel your feet supported firmly by the floor. Breathe deeply. Imagine that each breath you take calms and soothes you. The first breath you take goes to the very soles of your feet, the second breath fills your feet, the third goes directly to your ankles, the fourth settles in your lower calves, the fifth goes to your upper calves, the sixth to your knees . . ., and so on, until you are totally filled to the top of your head with new air. Continue breathing, and when it feels comfortable to you, open your eyes.

4. Take special care to drink eight to ten glasses of water per day during this period, particularly in a hospital environment, where the air tends to be dry. Water stimulates and energizes the body by helping to rid it of toxic waste.

5. It is good to cry. It is very good to cry.

6. It is okay to feel you hate Life/God/the Universe. Life/God/the Universe does not take this as a personal insult. It knows this feeling will—in time—pass for you.

Keeping Death A Secret

Because of its tender love and great understanding of the earth, the element of the person called "body" often doesn't want to leave. Sometimes . . . it takes time.

Yet there is a higher aspect of the loved one, the Life Force, that wills to move on, to make this transformation complete.

So, even if it has never been discussed, death is not a dark, painful secret—and the dying know that best.

Waiting are they? Waiting are they? Well, goddam 'em, let 'em wait!

—ETHAN ALLEN
(To his physician, who said, "General, I fear the angels are waiting for you.")

*In my Father's House are
many mansions.
I let go and allow my friend
to step into another room.*

I looked at the city of the living and said to myself, "That place belongs to the few." Then I looked upon the city of the dead and said, "That place, too, belongs to the few. Oh Lord, where is the haven of all people?"

As I said this, I looked toward the clouds, mingled with the sun's longest and most beautiful golden rays. I heard a voice within me saying, "Over there!"

—KAHLIL GIBRAN
(from "The City of the Dead")

3

During

The Light

I had seen my older brother a year before on an infrequent visit home to upstate New York. He was going on forty, and we joked about it. He was the type of guy who grows into forty handsomely. Physically strong and humanly kind. Some small lines around the eyes and dark hair graying slightly and evenly. He took my Mom and me to Thanksgiving dinner in his new truck, a Chevy I think—one of the sleek ones. Suede jacket, nice boots, good, neatly pressed jeans. I described him to friends in Los Angeles as the "upstate New York cowboy."

Now it was November 8th, almost a year since I realized he was handsome. He had been diagnosed only six weeks before—cancer. It wouldn't heal. He didn't look the same.

I was alone with him early that morning, and we held hands.

"Honey," he said, "you've got to help me."

"Tom, I am helping you. We're all helping you."

"But," he said, with a tense body and desperate eyes, "you've *got* to help me."

And I knew that it was happening. I thought of all the moments in the past few days I had wished it had happened when I wasn't there. Now it was happening — and I was very much there.

"Tom, I am helping you. We're all helping you. Can you feel us loving you and helping you?"

"No. God, help me . . . ."

"God is helping you, Tom. God is right here with you, helping you. You're safe. You're very safe. We're all here helping you. You *can* feel us helping you, can't you?"

He looked at me slowly and carefully. "Yes..., everyone . . . *is* helping me . . . ."

"Yes, we're all here helping you. You're safe. You're very safe."

He looked away, then back at me with the start of a smile.

"I'm safe . . . I *am* safe . . ., you're all doing a good job . . . ."

He was calmer now, still clutching my hand. We looked at each other for a long time.

"You're safe. You're very, very safe." I kept repeating.

"I'm safe . . . yes, I'm safe." Tom started to relax.

Then he put out his other hand and pulled me to his chest and hugged me with more strength than his weakened, skeletal form could possibly possess. The body bidding a strong farewell to the earth, and him saying goodbye to me.

My mother had been spending nights in his hospital room so he'd not be alone. Although she had just left the hospital when I arrived, I phoned her to come back.

Now I let *him* hold my hand, in case he wanted the freedom to let go.

"Tom, can you see the light?"

He seemed to look beyond me. Then, almost casually . . ., "Yeah . . . there it is. I can see the light."

"Tom . . ., can you go to the light?"

"Go to the light? Sure, I can go to the light."

There was no more effort. No more struggle. Suddenly the smile on his face was magnificent. He was so happy, so excited.

"I'm in the light! I'm in the light!"

He started clapping his hands, patting himself on the shoulder, smiling broadly. The tubes in his arm didn't exist for him anymore as he reached out to shake hands with people I couldn't see, then clap his hands some more.

The joy on his face beautified my world, and I started clapping too!

"Tom, what's happening?"

Nodding his head "yes," he kept smiling.

"They're doing this!" Clapping, patting his shoulder, shaking hands in the air.

There he was clapping and smiling with new light in his eyes, and I was clapping and smiling with happy tears in mine.

"Tom, is everyone there?"

"Yes, everyone."

"Is Daddy there?"

"Yes!"

"And Nana?"

"Yes. And Big Bud!"

I didn't know who Big Bud was until my mother later reminded me that, in his very early childhood, Tom was called "Little Bud" by our Uncle Andy, whom Tom called "Big Bud." Just something between the two of them. Uncle Andy had passed away years ago.

"Tom, is God there?"

"Oh . . .," he seemed to glance around," . . . probably."

Obviously, the seeming duality of Spirit and Matter, God and Man, was no longer Tom's concern. There was much more going on.

More clapping. Then a really big smile.

"Now they're getting ready. We're going to have a party for me—to celebrate."

He placed his hand on mine again.

"You're happy," I said.

"Oh yes, I'm very happy."

"It's very beautiful there, isn't it?"

It's *so* beautiful." He looked directly at me. "It's *extra special*."

He was very calm; his eyelids began to close. I began a litany of:

"You're very happy."

"You're very safe"

"It's very beautiful."

Over and over. He would say "yes" or nod his head or simply smile.

My mother arrived, and she witnessed this. She took my place at his bedside. He squeezed her hand.

About twenty minutes later, his body just didn't breathe anymore, and Tom was fully enjoying the party—his Celebration.

From Here To There

If you are with the loved one during the actual moments of passage from "here" to "there," you will know what to do. Have no concern about doing the "wrong" thing. With your love and compassion, nothing "wrong" can be done.

Remember that it is the loved one's process, transformation. It is the other person's show; you are an assistant. You need only be there, letting the person hold your hand if he or she wishes.

Do not think or presuppose that the person wants to die, doesn't want to die, that it is not time yet, or that it is past time. The loved one is totally in charge now and will proceed with the process in the best and proper way.

Just be there for the person. Let the loved one know you are there. Speak to the person clearly yet softly. If the person is young, and if you are able, hold the child on your lap, in your arms.

Do not try to hold the person's attention with words, but follow their lead. Tell the loved one often that he or she is safe.

If you feel comfortable using the image of moving to the "light," then, by all means, verbally support the person in going into the "light." If this does not seem comfortable to you, then use reassuring words of safety, comfort, beauty, and peace.

If the loved one is in a coma, speak anyway. A part of the person *can* hear.

If being alone with the loved one is too much for you to endure, ask for support and assistance from a family member, close friend, or from the hospital staff. You do not have to go through this experience alone.

Love the person who is dying. For the moment go a step beyond yourself and the human level of love that feels loss, feels pain. Look beyond the person's form and feel the love that Unifies all things. Know—tell yourself—that in this *true* love there can be no loss, no separation. There can be only love.

Breathe. Try to be aware of your breathing from time to time. This will still your mind, calm your thoughts.

When the Life Force of the loved one no longer needs to use the body as Its vehicle of expression here on earth, It will detach Itself, and the body will no longer breathe. With dignity, the soul has put the body to rest.

Do not call your loved one back. That Being is in the Divine Land now, safe from any worries and all harm.

The loved one has awakened from a dream the rest of us still share. Allow the part of you that *knows* this . . . to rejoice.

The Witness

As a witness or assistant in a transformation process, remember that it can be very tiring and draining for you.

All of you—your body, mind, emotions, Life Force—has been deeply involved in a death drama. Be aware that it is very natural and normal to feel exhausted and relieved at the same time. You may also be in shock.

Treat yourself well. Force yourself to do pleasant physical things immediately—a hot bath or jacuzzi, a good meal, an hour of rest, whether you sleep or not.

The death process is over for the loved one, but not for you. It is very important for you to care about yourself now.

This is a good time to use your personal journal or diary and write down:

—how you feel emotionally
—what you are thinking
—how your body feels

Write down in words anything you would like to express.

The Other Side Of Birth

When a baby is born, all parents feel a bit of anxiety about the infant's future: "Dear God, don't let anything happen to my child."

When someone dies, there can be no anxiety for the person's future, since the Life Force (God) can have no negative experiences.

Remember that those who die relearn, or remember, the secrets of Life that they forgot at birth.

So death, as the other side of birth, is remembering the glory of Immortality.

"Il n'y pas de morts."
(There are no dead.)

—MAURICE MAETERLINCK

I remember my loved one is a
Child of the Universe.
I get out of the way.
The Universe knows what to do.

I am standing on the seashore. A ship spreads her sails to the morning breeze and starts for the ocean. I stand watching until she fades on the horizon, and someone at my side says, "She is gone!"

Gone where? The loss of sight is in me, not in her. Just at the moment when someone says "She is gone," there are others who are watching her coming. Other voices take up the glad shout, "Here she comes!"

And that is dying.

—Anonymous

4

After

Life Goes On, Death Doesn't

When the transition process is completed for the loved one, it is not over for you. The immediate stress and tension of being with the dying person is now replaced by a period of grief.

You may feel some relief that the process is now finished and you may even say "it's a blessing." However, a grieving time certainly follows the death of a loved one and it can be harmful to deny yourself the days necessary to heal. The length of the grief or mourning period is personal for each individual, but the time does pass, the heartbreak does heal, the heavy sadness does lift. In time.

The beginning of the healing is tears. Crying is the body's expression of release. Crying releases feelings of sadness, anger, pain. Crying is your body's acknowledgment of what you are feeling and thinking, and enables you to begin to allow the grief to pass.

Give yourself permission to mourn.

As often as possible, during the days immediately following a death, be aware of what is happening to you. Practice catching your thoughts and feelings, and examine them. You don't have to change them, but be aware of what they are. Each day, in your personal journal or diary, write down the things you did or are going to do, how you feel, what you are thinking. This allows you to focus yourself back *into* your daily experiences.

The Ceremonies

If you are involved in any of the varied religious or social ceremonies for the dead, appreciate them as symbols of your loved one's movement into a higher life.

You may wish to perform your own private ceremony or ritual, in which, because of your love, you release the person to the new, better life he or she is now experiencing.

During any ceremony, it is important for you to be aware of your breathing. Although it is not necessary to constantly breathe deeply, it is a good idea to inhale and exhale completely, *i.e.*, complete each breath. Even remembering to do this occasionally will assist you in being clear in your thoughts and calm emotionally.

Anger, Guilt, And Grief

Very often, following a death, anger quickly rises up from nowhere and strikes out against another person, thing, or situation. This is mis-directed anger. We are *really* furious because a loved one died and left us.

This is normal and a natural step in our own healing process. Do not feel ashamed or embar-rassed because you are angry. The feeling will pass, as you allow it to pass and help it move along.

One of the best ways to get anger out of your physical system is to pound some pillows with your fists. It may seem silly or meaningless at first, but it is a physical action of anger that releases the emotion of anger.

You may also wish to write in your diary or journal just how angry you feel and why.

These suggestions do not dignify or reinforce your anger, they help you get rid of it.

Often you may experience a sense of guilt when a loved one passes away. This may be very subtle and difficult to pinpoint, but arises as a result of thinking you could have done something to change the outcome.

Know that there is *nothing* you could have done to change the outcome. You are not responsi-ble in any way for the loved one's death. That is a matter strictly between the person and the Universal Source of Life, or God.

The feeling of guilt is just a little part of your inner makeup trying to convince you that you are a bad person. You are not. You are a good person.

Select a piece of classical or soft music you especially enjoy, and play it. Sit quietly, with your eyes closed, and imagine that the music flows into your toes and all the way up through your body, then out your fingertips and out the top of your head. Each note of music washes you clean internally, and effortlessly eases any feelings that are not beneficial to you. Continue this until the piece of music ends. Do it again.

There may be moments when you feel as though you will die from the sadness. You may feel that the grief will never lift and the world will never again be bright for you. This is depression's "sledgehammer approach," and it is not at all subtle.

On a piece of paper or in your journal or diary, draw a picture of your heart—how it feels to you right now. You may want to color it. Then write down everything your heart is now feeling.

When you are finished, draw another picture of how you *want* your heart to feel. Then write down all the ways you *want* your heart to feel in the future.

Then write down five things you can do to help your heart feel better.

This activity helps to motivate you out of being stuck in deep sadness for too long a time.

Magic Moments

Trying not to be sad is using a great deal of energy in an attempt to deny an actual emotion. It is best to re-focus on something other than sadness. This removes your attention from the sadness, even if just for a few moments, and that allows the sadness to begin to fade.

It is impossible to "get rid of" the feeling of emptiness, but it is possible to fill the emptiness—then, it is not empty anymore.

Do something. Spend time doing something.

Some suggestions:

—dance/exercise class
—yoga
—good reading
—music lessons or playing an instrument
—shopping
—out for lunch or dinner
—sports, playing or watching
—movies
—visiting friends
—inviting friends to visit you
—going someplace you've never been: art gallery, museum, new mall
—spending some money on yourself
—joining a group of people who are helping each other through the time of bereavement
—taking a class in something that interests you
—volunteering a portion of time for a meaningful cause
—spending some time around children and animals
—gardening or potting new plants

Recent studies have shown that having a pet in the house—bird, fish, dog, cat, hamster, any pet—naturally lessens the length of time and the intensity of the mourning period.

Also, spending time in nature is both gratifying and healing. Be outside as often as you can. Air, sun, even rain and snow, heal.

Incorporating new activities into your days automatically enables grief to fade away.

There may be subtle elements of depression that seem to invade you when you least expect it. This need not be fought off, but can be recognized as small clouds that obscure the sun only for a few moments.

Realize that you do not have the burdensome task of "picking up the pieces" of your life. You have the freedom to design new pieces of your life that fit perfectly.

Grief exists because you are human and you have the ability to love others.

Grief fades because you are human and you have the ability to love others and to love yourself.

The Year That Follows

During the twelve months following the death of a loved one, there will be certain dates that will be significant to you. The loved one's birthday, or an anniversary, or a special day the two of you shared. Find a way to celebrate that day. Plan to do something that both expresses your love for the person who died and reinforces your own self-nurturing.

If there is a burial site, you may wish to plant or take flowers there, or even to your own home.

These "special days" can carry with them a certain amount of stress, so it is important to be very good to yourself.

If you are experiencing anger or depression or just the feeling that "something is wrong," it is a good idea to write a letter to the person who died. You can start by telling your friend how you feel, then go on by asking any questions you still may have regarding the person, events in the person's life, and even the transition itself. Conclude by telling the loved one of the events in your life at the moment.

When you have finished and re-read the letter, you may burn it, tear it up, or keep it safely in your journal or diary.

Some people may wish to wear a traditional symbol of mourning, such as a black arm band or ribbon, for a period of time. This symbol of wearing your emotion on your sleeve makes it easier for other people to understand what you are feeling. It can also aid in hastening the mourning period because it is a physical statement of sadness, and you will soon want to take it off and leave it off. This is an excellent sign of your healing.

Although the memory of your loved one is allowed to exist in all its intensity for whatever time you require, the first anniversary of the death can be marked by a Farewell Ceremony. This Ceremony is of your own design and can be as simple as taking a walk or lighting candles in your home or place of worship. You may want to attend a church service. Whatever you decide, take this time to talk to the person in your mind. Converse with the loved one in your imagination. Then, gently but firmly, let go. Let go.

Democracy of Death:
It comes equally to us all,
and makes us all equal when it comes.
—JOHN DONNE

*I do not deceive myself by
thinking I must suffer even
though I feel this sense of loss.
I remember that God loves me, and
therefore I love me too.*

And ye shall know the truth, and the truth shall make you free.

—JOHN 8:32

Humanity shows itself in all its intellectual splendor during this tender age, as the sun shows itself at dawn . . . .

—MARIA MONTESSORI

5

The Death of a Child

God, Patty, Me, And The Morning

by Patty's Mom

I brought Patty home from the hospital that night because we all knew there would be no morning for her. I had gotten all the necessary hospital permission and Patty was comfortable. As I held her in my arms in the rocking chair, I thought: wouldn't it be nice if tomorrow morning just never came? If there was simply no tomorrow? A devastating earthquake or a nuclear war—and the morning just didn't come for any of us? That would be nice.

I rocked back and forth, holding my sleeping/dying daughter. She had just turned six: three years living and three years dying. I talked to her softly, as we rocked through each hour of the night. I told her everything, as she slept with heavy breathing. I talked to her about love and beauty and the special gifts she brought to me. When my voice cracked, I would rest my head back and try to breathe without shaking. It was at those times I thought my own thoughts: how often did I cry so hard I would vomit? When did my husband and I really stop talking to each other? Did I still want desperately to kill God? Oh, how I so often wanted to kill God! Now, I decided it wouldn't be necessary to kill God *if* something wonderful happened during this night and there was no tomorrow morning. If we could all die with Patty, then I would let God live.

We rocked back and forth. Back and forth. I told my daughter about boys, and first grade, and the zoo. I quietly rambled on about things like ballet, water sports, and the Olympic Games.

At one point during the night I began to actually, somehow, *feel* that I was holding less and less of "her" to my heart. I rocked and cried and held her tighter.

Sometime later we just stopped rocking. In my head I could hear Patty telling me that "rocking is for babies" and "I'm a big girl now." I carried her to the couch, brushed back her hair, and covered her with a new Snoopy blanket—one she hadn't seen before. I held her hand.

"I'm a big girl now." I had to chuckle at the memory of a hospital visit last week (was it only last week?), when I arrived to find Patty and her little wing-mates all done up in lipstick, blush, and eyeshadow—playing "big girls" and giggling themselves silly!

I'm sure Patty knew I was thinking about this, because she smiled. Her eyes were closed, but she really smiled. And not a baby smile either. It was a warm, adult, loving smile, somehow filled with wisdom. My Patty was a big girl now. She was such a big girl that she let go of my hand.

I made the necessary phone calls. And I told God I changed my mind. Now that Patty was safe in another world, I needed the morning to arrive on this world, and I needed it very badly.

Even though I cried a lot, what was most important was that I could—and still can—see her beautiful, ageless, smile-of-wisdom and hear Patty's voice in my head saying "I'm a big girl now."

And as it has, and will, morning came.

A Child Is Dying

A child is terminally ill and is going to die. It simply makes no sense. It makes no sense at all. Please know that it also makes no sense to doctors, nurses, parents, and families throughout the world. Although this is a painfully unique experience for you, you are not alone when your child is dying.

All the questions can be answered and resolved, or unanswered and forgotten, in the years to come. Right now, you are in a special time, the most special time in your child's life, no matter how long you have been together. It is hard. And it hurts.

There is nothing in the world that holds greater promise than a young life. And when that young life is leaving *your* life, the sadness and grief may seem at times overwhelming and all-consuming.

Although it may seem unbearable, it is necessary now to maintain a sense of right action, or normalcy, in your daily life. Yes, your thoughts and love are centered on your child, yet it is important not to neglect Life itself. Communicate your thoughts and feelings to family members and special friends. This is not a time to shut out other loved ones. You may think that no one could ever understand the pain you are feeling; however, people will try to understand and support you, if you will let them.

During this critical time, ask and allow others to do things for you: grocery shop, clean the house, babysit other children, *etc.* You are going through a very demanding time and will benefit by turning some tasks over to others. The Universe is a strong and steady support system. Accept help now.

As with the pending death of any loved one, it is essential for you to take some time to nurture yourself. A warm bath, a walk in nature, a good dinner, even an exercise class, is not running away from your child. It is helping you lessen the stress of the days so you will be better equipped emotionally to spend time with your child. Even as you buy toys, games, books to bring to the hospital or sick room, try to buy a little something for yourself.

These things may sound so unimportant as you face the passing of a very special part of you. However, using some physical energy to nurture yourself acknowledges that *you* exist and fortifies your own well-being. Doing little things for yourself enables you to cope. And, please, try to remember to breathe. Several times a day, sit or stand and breathe deeply and evenly.

If your child is in a hospital or hospice, speak to the doctors and nurses. Ask any questions regarding your child that come to mind. Do not hesitate to question and even make suggestions regarding your child's comfort. The staff is there to assist patients and parents. And, although your child is his or her own authority in the transformation process, you are the adult in charge of life proceedings.

By all means, touch your child. We are all soothed by loving touch. Even if the child is asleep or in a coma, hold him in your arms, sing and talk softly to this, your child, this wonderful individual expression of an Infinite Universe.

No matter how old your child is, gently massage her hands, feet, and back. Touching is reassuring love. Make your child as comfortable as possible, and enliven the environment with colorful objects—pictures, toys, plants—things that your child's eyes enjoy seeing.

If your child is old enough to talk, please listen. Allow your child the freedom to express thoughts, feelings, even fears. Answer questions as honestly as you can. Laugh with the child; and smile at the child—often, often, often—with all the love in your heart.

If your child is asking you about sickness and death and you just *cannot* keep that conversation going, please ask for help from personnel, clergy, or counselors trained in death education.

You are very busy during this time, yet you may want to accept the assistance of a counselor for you and perhaps the entire family. A professional listener (therapist, psychologist, practitioner) for you to talk to—someone who is not involved in your daily life. You need not go through this alone.

However, when you are alone, there are things you can do. You can cry. You can feel the emotions as they seem to sweep over you. Write down what you are feeling. Use words, images, colors in your journal or diary, and let it all out.

In death, the body and soul lovingly release each other for the continual progression of that special expression, or aspect, of God you know as your child. You too need to release, as often as necessary, the feelings of pain, loss, confusion, even hatred, you may be experiencing. Putting it all in a journal, which you may either keep or later destroy, helps you release these feelings and assists you in beginning to heal the rest of your life.

You can also see the child in your mind, covered and surrounded in a bright, protective light. Sit comfortably at home, in the park, at the ocean, or in the room as the child sleeps, and close your eyes. Mentally picture your child enfolded in the color of joy. Focus your attention away from your present feelings, and give all your thought to the beautiful image of your child in total safety and perfect joy.

At another time, sit quietly and imagine the Universe (or God) as a huge, never ending, brilliantly cut diamond. See all the millions, even trillions, of shining facets in this perfect whole. All of your family members, friends, even strangers are each their own shining facet. Each is a part of the

Whole. So is your child a magnificent part of the Whole, part of the Universe, part of God. And, just as none of the shining facets can ever be lost or missing or even tarnished, neither can your child's life ever really end. The experience of life on earth may diminish and fade, yet Spirit-as-your-child continues forever as part of the Whole.

Just as you are, your child is a manifestation of Infinite Good here on earth. And although Infinite Good can change appearances, change forms, It can never die. The Infinite Universe holds you and your child, as you hold each other, in Its heart forever.

If it is possible, hold your child in your arms as he or she makes the final transition to a better life. Even if an infant, talk to your child, ease the life with words and touch through the short space of darkness into the light.

If this is impossible for you to endure, that is all right. You have already been proclaimed a very special person, since this child of Spirit had chosen you as Its parent here on earth. Whatever you do to assist the child in returning to a greater home, in awakening from the earth dream, is perfect.

When it is over, know that your child shines in the Mind of God, which is your Mind also. Lay your child's form to rest with the special dignity and love your son or daughter deserves.

I thank Life for sharing this child with me. We both loved well in the time we had together.

Sudden Infant Death

by Kate's Mom

My son is married now, and I'm about to be a grandmother. My daughter is in graduate school. My husband and I are doing very well; we are healthy and happy. I keep saying "My," "My," "My"—I sound so possessive! I think that's because you asked me to tell you about Kate—"My Kate."

My Kate, my firstborn, my baby. I was twenty-one years old and, oh what a joy! Married to the man I loved since high school and the mother of a beautiful baby. And she was such a good baby—healthy, smiling, kicking, and she hardly ever cried. I loved to look at her so much that I would check on her four or five times a night, just to see her and smile.

And it was on a Thursday night, or rather, early Friday morning, that I went in to check on her, and she was dead. Just like that. My Kate was not there anymore. A lifeless wax doll had taken her place. "My" baby was dead, and she didn't even cry goodbye.

It's not hard to remember. I cried and I hated. I hated myself, I hated my husband, I hated every baby I saw—even the ones on television commercials. It took time. I tried to love the memory of Kate, but after I stopped feeling "how could I have done this to my baby?," I started feeling "how could my baby have done this to me?" It was hard, and it was over twenty-five years ago.

I had to learn to love and accept love again. I had to learn to release Kate and still keep her in my heart. I had to learn to stop "blaming" myself and Kate. I had to learn that my identity is *me* and not "the mother of."

I still think of Kate and, it's funny, but throughout the years she has—sort of—grown with me. She never stopped being a part of my life, because she *was* an important part of my life.

The most important thing I learned is that love never stops. Oh, I know, for awhile after Kate was gone, I didn't feel much love . . . .

If it were possible, I would put my arms around every mother and father who has suffered a crib death. I would hold them tight and let them cry. I would tell them that the love never really stops and . . ., although I don't know how or when this happens . . ., life does become good again. They will wake up one morning and the memory of their baby will *not* be the first thing on their minds. I would promise them this. I know it is the truth.

Missing Children

> "If I could only know for certain that Mike was dead. He had been missing for two years. He would be fourteen now. I try to tell myself that he's dead so I can start to grieve for him. I even tried to go back coaching Little League this year, but driving to the school, I broke down and cried . . . again."
>
> —Mike's Dad

Where are they? Those little faces we see all around us these days under the words "Have you seen me?" Where are they? And why aren't they home?

The family and community grief surrounding the event of a missing child is enormous. It is also a double bind: we feel the anguish of the loss, but is mourning premature?

Please know that you are not willing your child dead by experiencing grief over his or her disappearance. You can keep hope alive by mourning for yourself. Do all that you find necessary to keep *your* life going.

Be in contact with the authorities and members of the community. This is not a time to hide your feelings, even your rage. Talk to people. If your voice is shaky, let it be heard anyway. You, and how you feel, are very important.

A missing child is not a quiet grief. It is an outrage reaching epidemic proportions in the United States. By communicating (telling family, friends, police, and civil authorities, other parents, children, the clergy, *etc.*, how you feel) you are helping to alter the mass-mind of a society where "children are missing every day."

This is one of the things you can do outwardly for your child, yourself, and your community.

And here, with love and compassion, you are urged caution. Do *not* take "the law" into your own hands. Doing so could range from meaningless to very harmful. Know that there is, within each of us and your child, a greater Law of Life in which nothing is ever lost or missing.

Child custody rulings may also include for you feelings of pain, confusion, and loss. Breathe. Try to bring to mind the greater Law of Life.

Use this Law for you and your child. Whenever—and every time—you see your child in your mind, surround him or her with the strongest, brightest light possible. This is not game playing, this is consciously focusing your attention of life and light. Even if you must force yourself, always see your child surrounded and protected by bright light. Supplant all terror images in your mind with the strong image of your child in the light of love. Include yourself in this light, with your child.

Use a journal or diary to put in writing how you feel. No one need ever read this. You can later burn the entries if you wish, but writing releases emotions, confusions, and fears. It helps to ease the pain.

Write letters in your journal to your child. Write many letters. Tell your child everything you are feeling. Ask the child questions.

Join other parents who are experiencing this same deep sadness. Even if, at moments, you may feel this is phony or fake, please know that by spending time with others you are adding a balance to your life that is much needed now.

Take care of yourself. Allow the waves of fear and emptiness to roll over you and fade away. Breathe. Whenever you think of it, stand still and breathe.

Reinforce your knowledge, even if you don't feel you "believe" it, that your child is safe in a Universe of protection and love. Focus your attention on living things with love and trust. Love and Trust.

Mourning The Loss Of A Child

Sadness
Hysteria
Nightmares
Confusion
Indecisions
Depression
Hostility
Low self-esteem
Hyperactivity
Mis/non-communications
Irritability
Inadequacy

Whether you are the mother or the father of a child who has died, the above list may define some of your present feelings and actions. You are not going mad, crazy, or insane. You are mourning the passing of a young one.

Somewhere inside you feel you birthed a baby to love and care for. And it died. The child, at whatever age, died before you did—and that was not what you expected of life. For reasons that seem unknowable right now, you have been dealt a nasty blow.

Grieve. It was not "just a child" and grief can never be measured by the size/weight/age of the one who moved on.

And you will not "just get over it," because you will now spend time working to live beyond it.

As you stand in your child's room and see the furnishings, toys, clothes, and special things, close your eyes and place your hand on your heart. Feel it beating. Feel the life that flows through you. Just stand quietly and feel your own heartbeat. Know that you are a living child of the Universe, and although this time may be very difficult for you, your heart will beat as the days pass. You will survive.

It may be very therapeutic and rewarding for you to donate your child's toys and other belongings to a children's home or to the children's wing at a hospital or hospice. In this way, the energy of your child's possessions is passed on to other children. A part of him or her continues to brighten the lives of others.

Use your journal to record and release the feelings of loss and betrayal. You may wish to write daily.

It is very important, now, that you do not build a wall around yourself. Talk to your family and friends. You may wish to have some regular sessions with a therapist trained in mourning counseling.

Take time for yourself. You will not forget your child, neither will you hold onto the pain of the child's absence. When you do not mask your mourning, you will not dwell on it.

Please incorporate the suggestions in Chapter 4 to help you move through and beyond the present sadness.

Mourning heals. Love yourself and allow it to happen. You show love and respect for your child when you continue to live your life, to let the days unfold as they will.

The Universe loves you. God loves you. And so it is.

Little Child, Big Soul

Know that this child is not a "poor little soul." This child is a resplendent acknowledgement of Life that can never die. The soul of a child is neither poor nor little. It is large, loving, beautiful, and healthy, just as the Source Itself.

The child came to teach and to learn. And, although it perhaps happened too quickly for you, the child has completed the mission. The child can now move on to even greater expressions of life and love. You and I have more to teach and more to learn.

Bless the child who graduates ahead of us.

Even if in tears, bless the child who finished his or her mission before the rest of us finished ours.

Take heart that you have loved and been loved by a very special aspect of God. Your child is always a precious part of Infinite Life, and so are you.

Rest, and be assured.

Today I carefully release any thoughts that God "took" my child. God gives, and my child accepts, a new and glorious morning.

. . . for you must go
and I must die.
But come ye back
when summer's in the meadow,
or when the valley's hushed and white with
snow.
For I'll be here
in sunshine and in shadow.
Oh Danny boy . . .
I love you so.

—Irish Folksong

6

Death in a Child's Life

For The Children

I was three years old when my grandmother died, and I still remember two things about the time:

- —I got to wear my new burgundy snow-suit to stop at the wake for a moment with my Mom.
- —I couldn't figure something out: Nana went to heaven to be happy with God, so why was everybody so sad?

The death of a family member, friend, or pet in a child's experience can be devastating or, as in my case, quite confusing.

Be aware of, and understand, your own feelings first, and be willing to tell the child how you feel. The child learns from you that emotions of sadness and feelings of loss are okay right now and that they will pass.

Hold the child in moments of his/her deep grief. Physical contact heals.

Tell the child the truth when questions are asked. If some questions are unanswerable ("But *why* did Grandpa die?"), tell the child you don't know, and explain that the question is a good one to ask and a hard one to answer.

You will want to encourage the child to express, often, how he or she is feeling about the death. Be sure the child is not harboring needless misunderstandings or blaming himself or herself for causing the death. ("I was bad, so Grandpa left me.")

Remember that anger is a part of grief—yours and the child's—and direct the anger into pillow pounding, discussion, and journal/diary writing.

This is an excellent time for the child—if old enough—to use the journal/diary to record thoughts and feelings.

The best way *not* to reinforce fear in the child is, first, to be open and honest about thoughts and feelings; second, to provide security for the child by explaining that no one was to blame and that no one could have changed the outcome; third, by teaching the child that the Life Force (or whatever term you prefer) of the person never dies and continues to love the child.

Concentrate on life. Do some "favorite things" or new activities together with the child.

My four-year-old friend, Yves, experienced the death of his kitten. He and his mother had a burial ceremony for the cat, and they discussed at length what death was all about. His mother was very careful to explain that it is okay to cry and feel sad for awhile. She held him, answered all his questions, encouraged him to express how he felt and what he was thinking. In the afternoon, she took him shopping. In the toy store, he let out a big sigh and said quietly to himself, "Oh, kitty!"

That instant was his healing. By nightfall, grief had passed and Yves was on the phone with me, telling me the story of kitty—how she died, and that he had been very sad, but now he felt pretty good because he knew that kitty was just "playing somewhere else."

Look to the children, not away from them. Be honest and fair. As you comfort them, know that they are comforting you.

Today I practice Love. I begin to heal
as I remember to forgive.

*The brevity of life, which is so constantly
lamented, may be the best quality it possesses.*

— ARTHUR SCHOEPENHAUER

*His dog up and died,
Up and died.
After twenty years,
He still grieved.*

"Mr. Bojangles"
BY JERRY JEFF WALKER

7

The Death of a Pet

Man's Best Friend

I raised Max from a ten-day-old, five-and-one-half-ounce kitten. He died at age two, weighing seventeen pounds. I was heartbroken. For the longest time, I would turn and see him—but he really wasn't there.

The loss of an animal in one's life can carry with it the same feelings as the loss of a beloved friend.

Since everything that lives is composed of energy, and energy can only be transformed, not destroyed, know that the energy or Life Force of the animal still exists, although its form does not.

Pets are our own reflections. They are dearly attuned to us, and we to them.

If a pet must be put to sleep in a Vet's office, try to stay with the animal. Stroke it, talk to it, ease it from "here" to "there."

If the pet is not in pain, but is fading at home, make it comfortable, warm, and provide water. It is not necessary to sit by the animal constantly, but don't ignore it either. Talk to the pet in a clear, gentle voice. Talk to it in your mind also. Avoid loud noises and don't disturb the pet by waking it.

Sit quietly and close your eyes. Select a color that represents to you warmth, safety, comfort, and peace. Imagine that you can cover the animal completely in this color. When you see it completely covered in this color, tell the pet in your mind that it is safe and peaceful. Love your pet in your thoughts. When it feels comfortable to you, open your eyes.

After the animal is gone, you may want to make up a private or family ceremony in which, with love, you release the pet's energy to its home in the Universe. Thank the pet for sharing its life with you.

In your journal or diary, write a letter to your animal. Tell the pet everything you want to say: how you feel, that you love the pet and miss it, that you feel sad, angry, *etc.* This is also a good idea for children to do when a pet has died.

Chances are you will find yourself mourning your pet with many of the same feelings as when a person dies. It is good to acknowledge and explore these feelings, just as it is very therapeutic to weep over the loss of a pet.

Allowing the feelings "out" enables them to fade faster.

By all means, when you feel comfortable about it, definitely get a new pet. Love brings more love, and there are many animals ready, willing and needing to love you back.

God never abandons Its creations;
therefore, I know my pet is safe at Home.

To fear death, gentleman, is nothing other than to think oneself wise when one is not; for it is to think one knows what one does not know. No man knows whether death may not even turn out to be the greatest of blessings for a human being; and yet people fear it as if they knew for certain that it is the greatest of evils.

—SOCRATES

"All of us loved him very much. With trust in God, we all pray that David has finally found the peace that he did not find in life."

—SENATOR EDWARD KENNEDY
(On the death of his twenty-nine-year-old nephew, David Kennedy)

8

Sudden Death

Shock

In the sudden death circumstance of a loved one, such as accidents, suicides, murders, war, the pain and confusion is often heightened because you are truly in shock.

It is very important to immediately start to take special care of yourself. Rest as much as possible, even if you don't sleep. Eat nourishing foods. Take warm baths. Allow your body to start releasing the shock/stress *first*. Then you can begin to handle the thoughts and emotions more clearly.

During the first few days following a sudden death, take five or ten minutes every two hours to sit or stand quietly and breathe deeply. Gently fill your lungs with air, then slowly exhale. Do this slowly, over and over again.

In a sudden death situation, very often thoughts arise such as:

"If I said _____ this wouldn't have happened."

"If I hadn't _____ this wouldn't have happened."

You must understand that you had *nothing* to do with it. **No One Dies Unless The Life Force Of That Person Agrees To Leave The Planet.** You may not know the reason, so do not blame yourself for another person's decision.

In your journal or diary, imagine you can have a conversation with the person who has died and write it out just as you would a script for a play. You are having a conversation in writing with this person. Write down a question then write down what the person "says" in response. Continue this until the written conversation comes to a natural ending.

You may also wish to write the person a letter asking all the unanswered questions you have on your mind. By asking the questions in writing, you are helping to clear your inner confusion.

As with the death of any loved one, a sudden death brings a time of mourning. However, you have been thrown into it now with no time to prepare.

Take very good care of yourself. Use the suggestions in Chapter 4 to help you deal daily with grief. Be willing to seek professional assistance, a therapist or counselor trained to help those in mourning.

Most important, know (and you already do know this somewhere within you) that the person who has made a transformation is safe and secure, free from pain, worry, fear.

The grief surrounding you will lift. In time it will be gone. One day—soon—you will feel the sun rising in your heart again.

I know it. So do you.

*I give myself the gift of
resting for just one moment,
in the peace of knowing that
God is all there is.*

Collective Consciousness And the Death of Strangers

*"The crew of the space shuttle Challenger
honored us by the manner in which they lived
their lives. We will never forget them, nor the
last time we saw them this morning as they
prepared for their journey and waved goodbye
and 'slipped the surly bonds of earth to touch
the face of God.'"*

—RONALD REAGAN

On January 28, 1986, the American space
vehicle Challenger exploded upon take-off from
Earth. Seven astronauts, seven living, active people,
died aboard the spacecraft.

But it is not exactly that they died, it is
that—quite simply, in the blink of an eye—they no
longer existed. They vanished. There was nothing
left. And we saw it on television.

Even with our Star Trek background of a
helpful, harmless "Beam me up, Scotty," a loss such
as Challenger affects humankind on many levels.
We have lost members of our family, whether we
knew them or not. The "death of strangers" is
perhaps more subtle than the passing of a loved one,
yet it is a loss we feel, and it is something to be
acknowledged.

When you read or hear or see the death of
others in accidents, wars, natural disasters . . ., how
do you feel? You certainly need not dwell on
catastrophe, but take a moment. Feelings of compassion, confusion, sadness, and even hurt are very

real to us when we experience, even via the newspaper, the death of others.

There is only one Infinite Intelligence, and we are *all* a part of that same Thing, or Life Force, if you will. Since all human beings can communicate with each other (in words, sign, movement, music, eye contact, and in thought), are we not, each then, responsible for what we communicate?

Race Mind, or mass thinking, is a very tricky thing. We have all, at one time or another, held a belief that was the result of thinking along with the masses. Thoughts such as "I get the flu every winter, everyone does," or "The economy is rotten, so we'll never have enough money," or even the basic "Blue is for boys, pink is for girls," are examples of mass thinking.

By taking responsibility for how we individually think, we can change our own thoughts and life experiences. And because there is only one Infinite Intelligence and we are all part of it, when we change our own thoughts to the positive, we are helping change the thinking of the entire race.

Think for a moment how you used to feel about the subject of death and dying. Is it possible now to accept the possibility that life always continues?

What do you think the prevailing Race Mind opinion is about death? Does the human race generally think that death is the end of everything? The cruelest cut of all?

Now, what makes you *feel* better, way deep inside: knowing that death is the final end or knowing that the energy of life always continues?

I do not deny the emotions involved in the loss of a loved one or a stranger, but I do support our knowing that the word "death" is just a short term for transformation or graduation from days spent on earth to the next better experience.

When a catastrophe occurs, there is a natural "collective mourning"—a national or international connectedness, expressing sorrow and grief for the victims. Now is the time to watch your thoughts. Now is the time to *know* in your mind and your heart that those who no longer live on earth have simply gone before us. They do not have more to learn or more to teach here. We do.

Infinite Love
extends beyond the Universe,
extends beyond death.

Poem for The Living

When I am dead
Pray for me a little,
Think of me sometimes,
But not too much.

It is not good for you
To allow your thoughts to dwell
Too long on the dead.

Think of me now and again
As I was in life,
At some moment that is pleasant to recall,
But not for long.

Leave me in peace
As I shall leave you, too, in peace.
While you live
Let your thoughts be with the living.

—Anonymous

Recommended Reading

General

Aries, Philip, *The Hour of Death.* Vintage Books (1982).

Bitzer, Robert H., *Ye . . . Shall be Comforted.* Church of Religious Science (1951).

Brady, Buff, *Endings.* Addison-Wesley (1979).

Capacchione, Lucia, *The Creative Journal: The Art of Finding Yourself.* Ohio University Press (1979)

Chaplin, Annabell, *The Bright Light of Death.* DeVorss & Co. (1977).

deBeauvoir, Simone, *A Very Easy Death,* Warner Paperback Library (1973).

Hay, Louise L., *You Can Heal Your Life.* Hay House (1985).

Kubler-Ross, Elisabeth, *On Death and Dying.* MacMillan (1969)

Kubler-Ross, Elisabeth, *Death: The Final Stage of Growth.* Prentice Hall (1975).

Kubler-Ross, Elisabeth, *To Live Until We Say Goodbye.* Prentice Hall (1978).

Kubler-Ross, Elisabeth, *Working It Through.* MacMillan (1982).

Le Shan, Eda, *Learning to Say Goodbye: When a Parent Dies.* MacMillan (1976).

Levine, Stephen, *Who Dies? An Investigation of Conscious Living and Conscious Dying.* Anchor Press/Doubleday (1982).

Levine, Stephen, *Meetings At The Edge.* Anchor Press/Doubleday (1984).

Meek, George W., *After We Die, Then What?* Metascience Corporation (1980).

Moffat, Mary Jane, *In The Midst of Winter: Selections From The Literature of Mourning.* Vintage Books (1982).

Moody, Raymond A., *Life After Life.* Bantam (1976).

Moody, Raymond A., *Reflections on Life After Life.* Bantam (1977).

Mumford, Amy Ross, *It Hurts to Lose A Special Person.* Accent Expressions (1982).

Mundy, Jon, *Learning to Die.* Spiritual Frontiers Fellowship (1973).

Neale, Robert E., *The Art of Dying.* Harper & Row (1976).

Osis, Karlis, and Haraldsson, Erlendur, *At The Hour of Death.* Avon Books (1977).

Price, Eugenia, *Getting Through The Night: Finding Your Way After The Death of A Loved One.* Dial Press (1982).

Rawlings, Maurice, *Before Death Comes.* Thomas Nelson Publishers (1980).

Steinpach, Richard, *How Is It That We Live After Death And What Is The Meaning of Life.* Grail Foundation of America (1984).

Temes, Roberta, *Living With An Empty Chair: A Guide Through Grief.* Irvington Publishers (1984).

Walsh, Michael; Moffat, Ronald; *et al., The Quality of Death.* Templegate Press (1980).

Children

Barbanell, Sylvia, *When A Child Dies.* Pilgrims Book Services (1984).

Buscaglia, Leo, *The Fall of Freddy The Leaf.* Holt, Reinhart & Winston (1982).

Capacchione, Lucia, *The Creative Journal for Children and Adolescents.* Box 5805, Santa Monica, CA (1981).

Donnelly, Katherine Fair, *Recovering from The Loss of A Child.* MacMillan (1982).

Grollman, Earl A., *Explaining Death To Children.* Beacon Press (1976).

Jackson, Edgar N., *Telling a Child About Death.* Hawthorn/Dutton (1965).

Kubler-Ross, Elisabeth, *On Children and Death.* MacMillan (1980).

Mumford, Amy Ross; Danhauer, Karen E., *Love Away My Hurt: A Child's Book About Death.* Accent Expressions (1983).

Rofes, Eric E., and The Unit at Fayerweather Street School, *The Kids Book About Death And Dying.* Little, Brown & Co. (1985).

Pets

Miller, Harry, "The Old Dog," from *The Common Sense Book of Puppy And Dog Care.* Bantam (1980).

Nieburg, Herbert A., and Fischer, Arlene, *Pet Loss, A Thoughtful Guide for Parents & Children.* Harper & Row (1982).

Pitcairn, Richard H., "Saying Goodbye: Coping with a Pet's Death," from *Dr. Pitcairn's Complete Guide to Natural Health For Dogs And Cats.* Rodale Press (1982).

The Monks of New Skete, "Facing the Death of a Dog," from *How To Be Your Dog's Best Friend.* Little, Brown & Co. (1978).

There are many more books available to help you in your personal experience, including volumes of poetry and case studies. Consult your library and local (including church) bookstores.

"In this sad world of ours, sorrow comes to all, and it often comes with bitter agony. Perfect relief is not possible, except with time. You cannot now believe that you will ever feel better. But this is not true. You are sure to be happy again. Knowing this, truly believing it, will make you less miserable now. I have had enough experience to make this statement."

—Abraham Lincoln

Organizations

Following are national organizations you may contact to obtain services in your region:

To assist with the pending death of a loved one:

Forum for Death Education and Counsel (FDEC)
2211 Arthur Avenue
Lakewood, Ohio 44107
216/228-0334

National Hospice Organization (NHO)
1901 N. Ft. Myer Drive
Suite 402
Arlington, Virginia 22209
703/243-5900

Foundation for Thanatology
630 W. 168th Street
New York, New York 10032
212/694-4173

Living/Dying Project
PO Box 5564
Santa Fe, New Mexico 87502

To fulfill the dreams of terminally ill children:

A Wish With Wings
PO Box 110418
Arlington, Texas 76007
817/261-8752

Brass Ring Society
7020 S. Yale Avenue
Suite 103
Tulsa, Oklahoma 74136
918/496-2838

To assist parents and families with a sudden infant death:

National Sudden Infant Death Syndrome Foundation
Two Metro Plaza
Suite 205
Landover, Maryland 20785
Toll-free: 800/221-SIDS

To assist with finding missing children and to counsel parents:

National Center for Missing and Exploited Children
1835 K Street N.W.
Washington, DC 20006
202/634-9821
Toll-free Hotline: 800/843-5678

Missing Children—Help Center
410 Ware Boulevard
Suite 400
Tampa, Florida 33619
Toll-free: 800/USA-KIDS

Child Find
PO Box 277
New Paltz, New York 12561

Childsearch
Six Beacon Street
Boston, Massachusetts 02108
617/720-1760

To assist families and friends with accidents and suicide:

Mothers Against Drunk Driving (MADD)
669 Airport Freeway
Suite 310
Hurst, Texas 76053
817/268-6233

Parents of Suicides
15 East Brinkerkoff Avenue
2nd floor
Palisades Park, New Jersey 07650
201/585-7608

Seasons: Suicide Bereavement
4777 Naniloa Drive
Salt Lake City, Utah 84117

In addition, please inquire at your local hospitals and churches. There are many on-going programs to assist you in recovering from grief. You do not have to go through this alone. Others love you.

AS SOMEONE DIES, by Elizabeth A. Johnson, *a Hay House publication, is set in Paladium type; book design and production by* Susan C. Sennett; *graphics and cover design by* Doug Doyle; *typesetting by* Highpoint Type and Graphics, Inc., *Pomona, California; printed by* Delta Lithograph Co., *Valencia, California. Editorial and production consultant,* James Neyland.

The author expresses her gratitude to Laura Hale *for her contribution to this book.*